How Do Our Ears Hear?

Carol Ballard

RSVP

RAINTREE
STECK-VAUGHN
PUBLISHERS
The Steck-Vaughn Company

Austin, Texas

How Your Body Works

How Do Our Eyes See?

How Do Our Ears Hear?

How Do We Taste and Smell?

How Do We Feel and Touch?

How Do We Think?

How Do We Move?

Published by Raintree Steck-Vaughn Publishers, an imprint of Steck-Vaughn Company

Library of Congress Cataloging-in-Publication Data
Ballard, Carol.
How do our ears hear? / Carol Ballard.
p.   cm.—(How your body works)
Includes bibliographical references and index.
Summary: Introduces the parts of the ear and explains how they help us to hear sounds.
ISBN 0-8172-4737-8
1. Hearing—Juvenile literature.
2. Ear—Juvenile literature.
[1. Hearing. 2. Ear. 3. Senses and sensation.]
I. Title. II. Series.
QP462.2.B35   1998
612.8'5—dc21   96-9063

Printed in Italy. Bound in the United States.
1 2 3 4 5 6 7 8 9 0 02 01 00 99 98

Picture acknowledgments
The authors and publishers thank the following for use of their photographs: Chapel Studios 5(top), 14, 16; Chris Fairclough Colour Library *cover*, 4, 23, 27; Robert Harding 6, 10; Hearing Dogs For The Deaf 25; Popperfoto 29; Teletec International 24; Zefa 5(bottom), 22, *contents page*. The remaining pictures are from the Wayland Picture Library. **Illustrators:** Kevin Jones Associates and Michael Courtney. Art on page 26 by Kieran Walsh

Contents

Ears

Our ears are very important. We use them all the time to hear what is happening around us.

▲ We use our ears to listen to the sounds of the natural world.

We hear many different types of sounds. Some give warnings, like fire and smoke alarms. Some sounds give information, like the announcements at airports and railroad stations, news bulletins, and weather reports. Alarm clocks wake us, and telephones ring to let us know someone wants to talk to us.

We listen to the radio and television for pleasure. Although a television has pictures, you also need the sound. Try watching your favorite television program with the sound turned off and see what a difference it makes.

We use sound to communicate. We tell each other stories and jokes and listen to each other's problems and secrets. This book will tell you more about your ears and how they work.

Our ears allow us to ▶ hear friends on the telephone.

Parts of the Ear

Each ear has three sections: the outer ear, the middle ear, and the inner ear.

The outer ear consists of flaps on each side of your head called pinnae. They are made of cartilage, a strong, flexible material, that is covered with a layer of skin. Each pinna acts like a funnel, channeling sounds into the ear.

◀ Elephants have enormous ear flaps to help keep them cool.

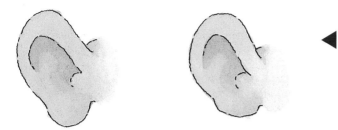

Look at your earlobes in a mirror. Are they curved or flat? Compare them with the earlobes of your family and friends.

The bottom part of each pinna is called the lobe. It is softer than the rest of the pinna because it does not have any cartilage inside. Some people have curved earlobes, and others have flat earlobes. The shape of your earlobe is **inherited**, in the same way as the color of your eyes and hair.

The rest of the outer ear is a tube called the auditory canal. Sounds travel along this tube to reach the middle ear.

skull bone

7

The outer ear ▶

pinna

earlobe

auditory canal

The Middle Ear

The middle ear is a tiny space filled with air. It is less than one inch (20 mm) high and $^1/_4$ inch (5 mm) wide. It is separated from the outer ear by the eardrum.

The eardrum is a thin sheet of skinlike material. It is stretched across the end of the auditory canal and is attached to a ring of bone.

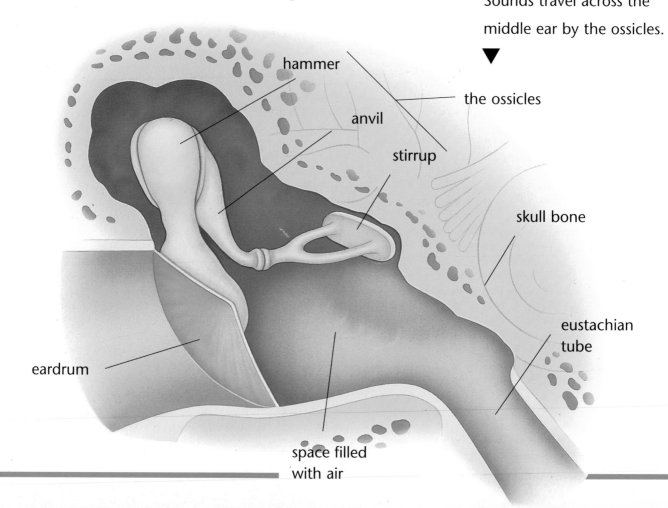

Sounds travel across the middle ear by the ossicles.
▼

hammer

anvil

the ossicles

stirrup

skull bone

eustachian tube

eardrum

space filled with air

Inside the middle ear are the three smallest bones in the body: the hammer, anvil, and stirrup. Together these are called the ossicles. They are linked together to form a chain of levers and are held in place by muscles and cords.

▲

Your ears pop in an airplane because the air pressure changes, and the eustachian tube opens with a "pop" when you swallow.

9

The middle ear is linked to the space at the back of your nose by a tube. This tube is usually closed, but air can pass through it when it opens. This keeps the **air pressure** inside the middle ear the same as the pressure outside.

The thin eardrum is stretched tight like ▶ the skin on the top of a drum.

The Inner Ear

The inner ear is a complicated network of spaces and tubes, all filled with liquid.

The inner ear is separated from the middle ear by the oval window and the round window. These are very thin sheets of skinlike material stretched tightly across two gaps in the skull bone. They keep the liquid inside the inner ear and keep air out.

▲
The inner ear is sometimes called the labyrinth because it is like a **maze** of tubes. The labyrinth was a complicated maze. According to Greek legends, a monster called the Minotaur lived at the center of it.

◄ The spiral cochlea is like a snail's shell. It gets its name from the Greek word for snail, kokhlos.

The cochlea is a coiled, bony tube filled with liquid. It is lined with tiny hairs that play an important part in hearing. They are linked to the auditory nerve, which carries messages from your ear to your brain.

Also in your inner ear are three loops called semi-circular canals. They are attached to a sac called the utricle. These do not help you hear, but they play an important part in keeping your body balanced.

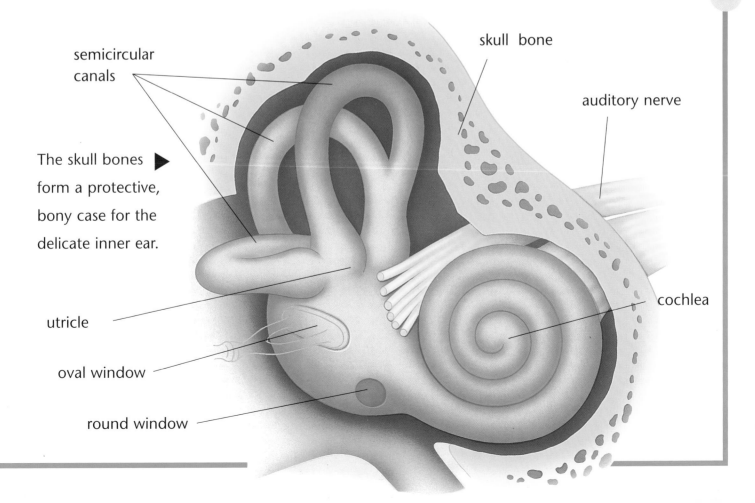

semicircular canals

skull bone

auditory nerve

The skull bones ▶ form a protective, bony case for the delicate inner ear.

utricle

cochlea

oval window

round window

How Do Ears Work?

A sound is a very tiny movement in the air, called a **sound wave**. To hear a sound wave, it has to travel through your outer, middle, and inner ear.

12

1. Your pinnae channel sound waves into your ears.

2. The sound wave travels along the auditory canal.

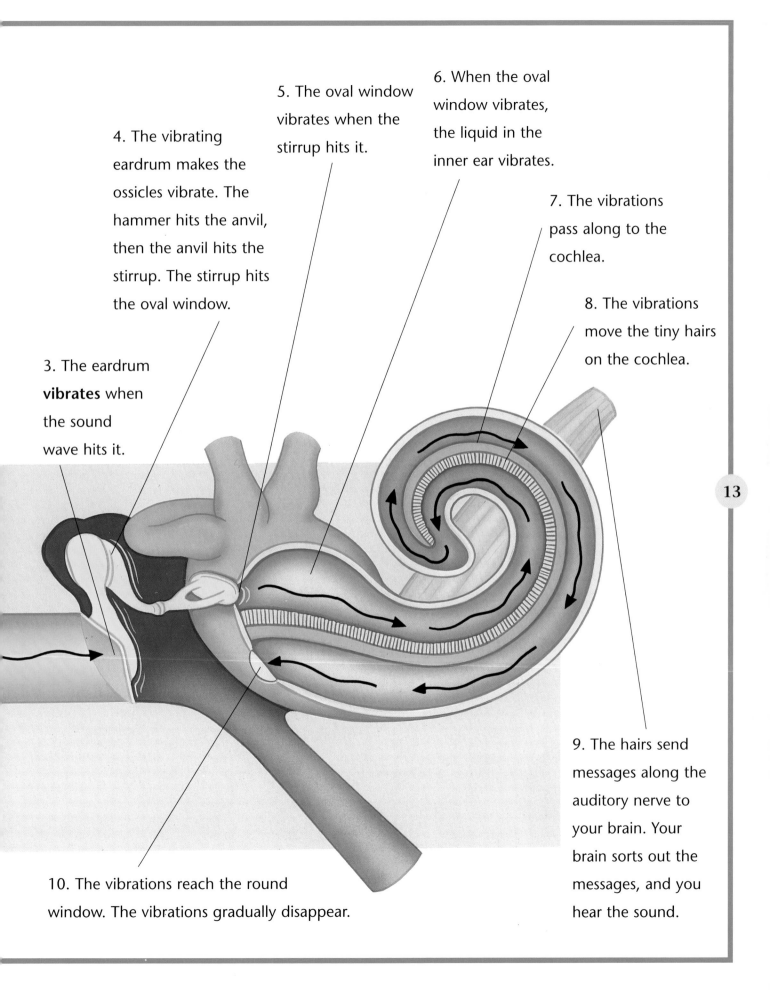

4. The vibrating eardrum makes the ossicles vibrate. The hammer hits the anvil, then the anvil hits the stirrup. The stirrup hits the oval window.

5. The oval window vibrates when the stirrup hits it.

6. When the oval window vibrates, the liquid in the inner ear vibrates.

7. The vibrations pass along to the cochlea.

8. The vibrations move the tiny hairs on the cochlea.

3. The eardrum **vibrates** when the sound wave hits it.

9. The hairs send messages along the auditory nerve to your brain. Your brain sorts out the messages, and you hear the sound.

10. The vibrations reach the round window. The vibrations gradually disappear.

Hearing Different Sounds

Think about some of the sounds you hear. Some, like birds singing, are high, and others, like thunder, are low. The range of high to low in sounds is called "pitch."

We can hear a wide range of pitch, but some sounds are too high or low for our ears to detect. Some other animals can hear them—there are dog whistles that can be heard by dogs but not by humans.

small wave pattern

large wave pattern

▲
Different sounds have different wave patterns. Loud sounds have larger waves than quiet sounds.

◀ The thicker the string, the lower the sound it makes.

High-pitched sounds have waves very close together. Low-pitched sounds have waves farther apart. The inner end of the cochlea responds to the close wave patterns of high notes. The outer end of the cochlea responds to the spread-out wave patterns of low notes.

Loud sounds have larger waves than quiet sounds, so they make larger vibrations inside your ear. Messages from your cochlea to your brain tell it how big the vibration was, so your brain can figure out how loud the sound is.

Do these musical instruments ▶ make high or low sounds? (A clue: the bigger the instrument, the lower the sounds it will make.)

Loud and Soft

The loudness of a sound is called its intensity. It is measured in **decibels**. We cannot hear a sound quieter than 0 decibels: this is the "threshold" of our hearing. Sounds can be quieter than 0 decibels, but our ears are not able to detect them.

Loud noises can damage our ears. People who use noisy equipment wear ear protectors to keep their ears from harm. Loud music can damage our ears, too.

◀ This woman wears ear protectors so her ears don't hear the noise of the machinery.

Find out about the noises around you by carrying out a sound survey. Use your classroom, playground, and street. At each place stand still for five minutes. Record the sounds you hear on a tape recorder or on paper. (You might need to decide on a code so it will not take too long.) Look at your results to see which was the quietest place and which was the noisiest place.

17

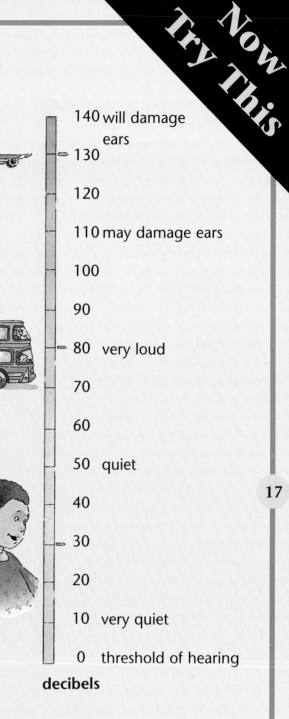

140	will damage ears
130	
120	
110	may damage ears
100	
90	
80	very loud
70	
60	
50	quiet
40	
30	
20	
10	very quiet
0	threshold of hearing

decibels

▲

Record the sounds from your sound survey on a chart like this.

Balance

The three semicircular canals and the utricle in the inner ear help the body stay still when we are sitting or standing, and to balance when we are moving about.

▲

Travel sickness is caused by the brain's receiving two different messages. The eyes tell the brain you are moving while the inner ears tell the brain you are still. To keep from feeling sick, look ahead at the horizon so that your eyes will be still.

Inside each canal is a structure like a swinging door. When you move your head, the liquid inside the canals pushes these doors open or shut. Tiny hairs inside the canals and the utricle detect this movement and send messages to your brain. The brain uses this information to figure out the new position of your head.

Have you ever spun around and around and then felt dizzy when you stopped? The liquid inside the utricle cannot stop as quickly as your head. It keeps moving for a few seconds, so your brain still gets messages from it after you have stopped spinning.

Each canal lies in a different direction: up and down, right and left, and back and front. ▼

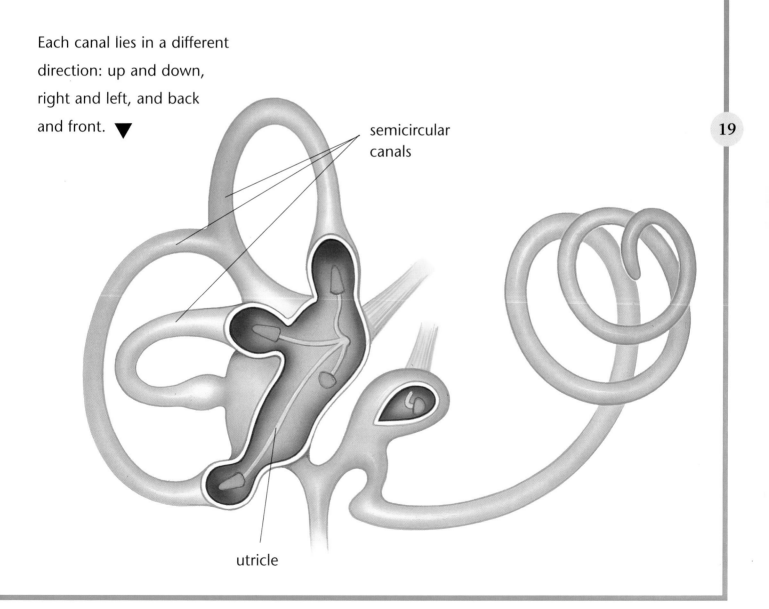

semicircular canals

utricle

Using Two Ears

Have you ever wondered why you have two ears and why one is on each side of your head?

▲
Some animals can move their ears independently of each other to help pinpoint exactly where a sound is coming from.

Having two ears helps tell the direction a sound has come from. A sound will reach one ear a fraction of a second before it reaches the other. It will also be a tiny bit louder in one ear than in the other. The brain puts the information from both ears together and figures out where the sound came from.

Try finding the direction of a sound. Ask a friend to blindfold you and then to move a few steps away. Make a noise, like clapping hands. Ask your friend to make this noise from different positions. Can you tell exactly where your friend is? Now repeat the test, first with your left ear covered and then with your right ear covered. Can you still tell where your friend is?

These children are trying to ▶ find out if two ears are better than one.

How Well Can You Hear?

Not being able to hear properly can cause problems with learning. Doctors and health workers test how well babies and young children can hear, but unless the problems are serious they are often not noticed until a child starts school.

▲

Ear trumpets were used before modern hearing aids were invented. They acted as enormous pinnae, channeling more sound waves into the ear.

◄ A doctor may use a special instrument to check a baby's hearing.

A hearing specialist checks whether a child can hear high and low sounds, and loud and quiet sounds. Then the specialist tries to find out why the child cannot hear properly. He or she checks to see whether the outer ear is blocked and may also examine the eardrum using a special instrument called an otoscope. An otoscope shines a light into the ear and allows the middle ear to be seen. Any signs of infection or other problems can be spotted.

As they get older, many people suffer gradual loss of hearing. They may decide to get a hearing aid.

These girls are deaf, so ▶ they use hearing aids and **sign language**.

Deafness

Deaf people need special help so that they can lead independent lives. Machines are designed to help deaf people do everyday activities. They may use a telephone with a printer that writes what the caller says. A light may flash when somebody presses the doorbell. Deaf people may use hearing aids. These are tiny microphones that fit inside the ear and make sounds louder.

24

◀ The screen on this telephone lets a deaf person see what the caller is saying.

Some deaf people have "hearing dogs." These dogs are trained to alert their deaf owners to sounds such as doorbells, telephones, and alarm clocks. Instead of barking, the dogs are taught to touch their owners and then lead them to the sound.

Many deaf people can understand what other people are saying by lip reading. They watch carefully as people talk, and figure out what is being said from the shapes and movements of their lips.

A hearing dog can help a ▶ deaf person do things we take for granted.

Sign Language

Many deaf people use sign language to help them communicate with other people.

Sign language has been used for hundreds of years. In medieval monasteries monks in "silent" orders were not allowed to speak, so they used sign language to communicate with one another. There are still some monasteries like this today.

A

B

C

D

Here the first four letters of the hand alphabet can be seen. ▶

◀ These children are using sign language.

There are two types of signs, those for whole words and those for single letters. Words that are used a lot have their own signs. These are often **gestures** that we use naturally, like a shiver to say "cold," "thumbs up" to say "OK," and shrugging shoulders to say "I don't know."

Words that are not used often do not have their own signs. Instead, they have to be spelled out one letter at a time, using an "alphabet" of finger and hand positions.

Children who are born deaf often find it difficult to learn to talk. Their teacher may use sign language instead of talking to them.

▼

Take Care of Your Ears

It is important to take care of your ears. Here are some suggestions about how to keep your ears healthy.

Try to keep them clean. Never stick anything in your ear because it could get stuck or hurt your eardrum.

▲

You may enjoy loud music but it is not good for your ears.

Loud noises can damage your ears, so try to avoid them if you can. When listening to a compact disc player, make sure the volume is not too high. Try not to use earphones for long spells without a break. Avoid spending too much time in very noisy places.

If you take part in an activity where ear protection is provided, then make sure you use it.

If you have had problems with your ears, follow the advice of your doctor. You may have to stop activities like swimming for a while, but this may only be for a short time, and your ears have to last you a lifetime.

It can be noisier at a rock concert ▶
than in some factories.

Glossary

air pressure The force of air pushing against something.

decibel The measure of how loud a sound is.

inherited Passed down from your parents.

gestures Movements of the hands, head, or body to show feelings.

maze A path or passage designed to confuse those walking through it.

sign language A system of gestures, instead of speech, used by deaf people.

sound wave The movement of sound through air.

vibrate To move back and forth very quickly.

Books to Read

Greenaway, Theresa. *Ears & Eyes*. Head to Tail. Austin, TX: Raintree Steck-Vaughn, 1995.

Rauzon, Mark J. *Eyes & Ears*. New York: William Morrow & Co., Inc., 1994.

Savage, Stephen. *Ears*. Adaptation for Survival. New York: Thomson Learning, 1995.

Showers, Paul. *Ears Are for Hearing*. New York: HarperCollins Children's Books, 1993.

Snell, Nigel. *Hearing*. Senses. North Pomfret, VT: Trafalgar Square, 1991.

Index

32